Programmed to Run

Programmed to Run

Thomas S. Miller, PhD

Human Kinetics

Library of Congress Cataloging-in-Publication Data

Miller, Thomas S., 1942-
    Programmed to run / Thomas S. Miller.
       p. cm
    Includes bibliographical references (p.) and index.
    ISBN 0-7360-3749-7
    1. Running. I. Title.

    GV1061 .M49 2002
    796.42--dc21

                                                2001039553

ISBN: 0-7360-3749-7

Acquisitions Editor: Martin Barnard; **Developmental Editor:** Laura Hambly; **Assistant Editor:** Kim Thoren; **Copyeditor:** Karen L. Marker; **Proofreader:** Susan C. Hagan; **Indexer:** Daniel A. Connolly; **Permission Manager:** Toni Harte; **Graphic Designer:** Robert Reuther; **Graphic Artist:** Francine Hamerski; **Photo Manager:** Tom Roberts; **Cover Designer**: Keith Blomberg; **Photographer (cover):** David Madison; **Photographer (interior):** Tom Roberts, unless otherwise noted; photo on page vi © Bongarts/SportsChrome USA; photo on page 22 © David Madison/Bruce Coleman, Inc.; photos on pages 34–37 courtesy of Tom Miller; photo on page 46 © Dugald Bremner; photo on page 80 © Victah Sailer; **Art Manager:** Craig Newsom; **Illustrator:** Dody Bullerman; **Printer:** Bang Printing

Human Kinetics books are available at special discounts for bulk purchase. Special editions or book excerpts can also be created to specification. For details, contact the Special Sales Manager at Human Kinetics.

Printed in the United States of America   10 9 8 7 6 5 4 3 2 1

Human Kinetics
Web site: www.humankinetics.com

United States: Human Kinetics
P.O. Box 5076
Champaign, IL 61825-5076
800-747-4457
e-mail: humank@hkusa.com

Canada: Human Kinetics
475 Devonshire Road Unit 100
Windsor, ON N8Y 2L5
800-465-7301 (in Canada only)
e-mail: orders@hkcanada.com

Europe: Human Kinetics
Units C2/C3 Wira Business Park
West Park Ring Road
Leeds LS16 6EB, United Kingdom
+44 (0) 113 278 1708
e-mail: hk@hkeurope.com

Australia: Human Kinetics
57A Price Avenue
Lower Mitcham, South Australia 5062
08 8277 1555
e-mail: liahka@senet.com.au

New Zealand: Human Kinetics
P.O. Box 105-231, Auckland Central
09-523-3462
e-mail: hkp@ihug.co.nz

This book is dedicated to all those runners who have endured my compulsive coaching throughout the years. I am especially grateful to Wendy Riser Van de Kamp, John Cahill, and Debbie Moss, who encouraged, supported, and inspired me to stick with it through all the rejections, revisions, and drudgery associated in completing this seemingly life-long project. Finally, I dedicate this book to those of you reading my work for the first time. I hope it will inspire you to become students of running and teachers of runners, just as I was inspired by the early writing of long-time *Runner's World* editor and writer, Joe Henderson. He taught me that the joys of running are not limited to the talented, but available to everyone.

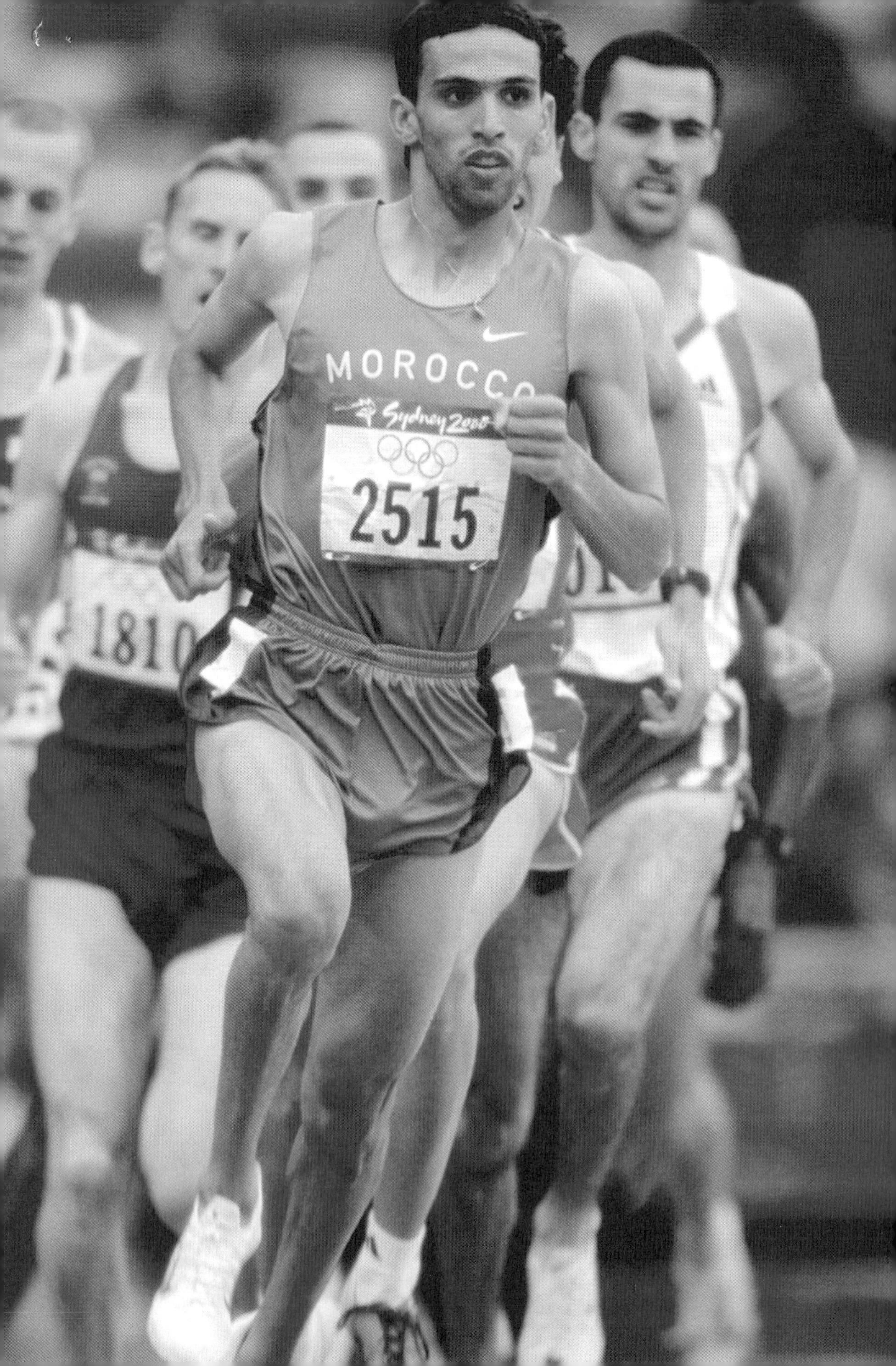
MOROCCO
Sydney 2000
2515
1810